King Frank

by Ethan Cruz
illustrated by Benton Mahan

Core Decodable 58

Bothell, WA • Chicago, IL • Columbus, OH • New York, NY

MHEonline.com

Copyright © 2015 McGraw-Hill Education

All rights reserved. No part of this publication may be reproduced or distributed in any form or by any means, or stored in a database or retrieval system, without the prior written consent of McGraw-Hill Education, including, but not limited to, network storage or transmission, or broadcast for distance learning.

Send all inquiries to:
McGraw-Hill Education
8787 Orion Place
Columbus, OH 43240

ISBN: 978-0-02-138170-8
MHID: 0-02-138170-4

Printed in the United States of America.

2 3 4 5 6 7 8 9 DOC 20 19 18 17 16 15

King Frank rested.

He rested in the garden.

Sir Quint hushed the men.
"King Frank must rest."

Sir Quint hushed the kids.
"King Frank is resting."

Then a problem happened.
Bang! Bang! Bang! Clank!

"What is that banging and clanking?"
Sir Quint said, "That must stop this second!"

Bang! Bang! Bang! Clank!
Sir Quint ran to the men.

"Quit banging!" said Sir Quint.
But the men did not bang.

Bang! Bang! Bang! Clank!
Sir Quint ran to the kids.

"Quit clanking!" said Sir Quint.
But the kids did not clank.

Sir Quint did a bit of quick thinking.

Sir Quint ran to the garden.
Bang! Bang! Bang! Clank!

King Frank had a ball.
Bang! Bang! Bang!

King Frank had a long shot!
Clank! He missed his shot.

Sir Quint grinned.
King Frank was not resting.